WORLD TRAVEL
AND A
HISTORY OF TOILETS

JANE SCHAUER

Written and illustrated by Jane Schauer.
This third edition published in 2011
by KREAV Publishing,
Canberra, Australia.

ISBN 978-0-9804633-6-1

KREAV PUBLISHING

WORLD TRAVEL AND A HISTORY OF TOILETS

Jane Schauer was born in London and has travelled widely. She now lives in Canberra, Australia with her husband Cyril, several wild possums and her cats, Junior, Scampey and Mother Cat.

Jane in Tolkien's old study at
Exeter College, University Of Oxford.

World Travel And A History Of Toilets

This book is for Cyril (because it's the only thing I have ever written that he likes) and for the gang at the Oxford University Summer Programme in Creative Writing, who laughed and clapped when I read them excerpts.

World Travel And A History Of Toilets

The word toilet is confusing because it can have any or all of three meanings. In the past it meant the acts of grooming and cleanliness, such as washing your hands, or having a shave. Now it usually means the room where you excrete, or the flushable device into which you excrete.

"You can go into the toilet to sit on the toilet in order to go to the toilet and then afterwards you can do your toilet. When you have finished you can take some toilet water out of your toilet bag and sprinkle yourself with it."

The world toilet day is Nov 19th of every year. The World Toilet Organisation has said the purpose of the day is to have people take action to increase awareness of toilet user's right to a better toilet environment. The organisation holds an annual summit.

You can visit their website for details.
www.worldtoilet.org

World Travel And A History Of Toilets

Chapter One
Money Doesn't Stink

Most people who are not Australians think that Sydney is the capital of Australia. It's not, it is Canberra - my home town. In Canberra it's very cold in winter, so I was pleased to avoid the cold by travelling overseas to warmer places. I planned to visit some scenic places and do some interesting things. I did not realise that toilets would become such a significant part of my grand tour around the world.

Australian towns have clearly marked public toilets, service stations have toilets for customers, national parks and remote highways have modern composting toilets. Surprisingly the composting loos don't smell or even subject you to the distasteful experience of having to look at what is already composting - unless you are really interested.

A composting toilet works by organic decomposition. Modern ones are self-contained, waterless and odourless. Chemicals are not used. Wood chips or grass clippings assist the composting. Safe compost is the end result.

Composting Toilet

Toilet Etiquette

Modern toilet etiquette varies depending upon country and religion. Islamic etiquette can be quite complex and can involve the following:

- Entering the toilet with the left foot and leaving with the right, and saying specific words when entering and leaving the toilet
- Not standing or talking whilst going to the toilet
- Facing the correct direction and ensuring privacy when going to the toilet
- Performing a specified washing ritual afterwards

Public toilet etiquette rules for men in the West are:

- If you don't want to be interpreted as making homosexual advances, don't make eye contact with other men or stare at their genitals

- Choose a urinal as far as possible away from any being used
- If women also use the toilet, then lower the seat after using a pedestal type toilet

Public toilet etiquette rules for women in the West are:

- Wipe off any splashes on the toilet seat and always flush
- Be as quick as you can on planes, and in other similar situations, where others are waiting to use the small toilet room which also contains the washing sink (e.g. don't spend half an hour in the room applying your make-up while others are waiting)

Some public toilet etiquette rules for both sexes are:

- Don't talk
- Try to minimize body noises when going to the toilet

We are well toileted in Australia, so I was not prepared for the United States. Driving through Massachusetts with Cyril there were no toilets to be seen. Eventually, as he crazily zig-zagged across Massachusetts (because he kept missing our turn) I was able to answer the call of nature. We stopped to get petrol, or gas as it is called in the States. On the counter was a sign saying "No Public Toilet". But I begged and received permission to use their private toilet. It was dingy and didn't have a door.

Usually you say "rest room" or "bathroom" in the States, rather than toilet, because that is what toilets are euphemistically called. Years ago, when I first visited my mother-in-law in Saint Louis, I asked where the toilet was. She looked at me as if I had said an obscene word and she icily insisted I wanted the bathroom. She then showed me to the toilet, which was next to the bathroom.

Cyril and I stayed in an apartment in Boston. I had rented it from a web-site that promised the apartment would be very luxurious, including having a jacuzzi in which we could relax. What we got was an apartment cluttered with run-down furniture, including 24 chairs, a jacuzzi that could only be filled with cold water that came from a large hole in the ceiling above it and décor that consisted of 35 pictures of nude men or boys. However, the apartment did have three toilets.

After staying in Boston, Cyril and I drove around the charming, narrow roads of the Cape Cod area. The streets were leafy, the flowers in bloom, and the picturesque Cape Cod homes looked almost cloyingly beautiful. We stopped at a large second-hand book store and I bought a rare book on the medicinal uses of Scottish herbs and seaweeds. Just inside the entrance door of the bookstore was a sign "No Public Toilet".

I frequently saw that sign as we drove around, but I never saw any sign saying "Public Toilet". Perhaps one of the reasons that Americans love going to shopping malls, restaurants and bars is simply that they can go to the toilet.

There has been a long history of public toilets and there has also been a long history of meanness. The Roman Emperor Vespasian (ruled 67-79AD) ordered that there be a charge for the use of public toilets. When criticised he said that "money doesn't stink".

There are some really mean aspects of private enterprise in the United States. One is the fact that most of the beaches are private and off limits to the public. So it was wonderful to discover the huge Cape Cod National Seashore Park with lots of fabulous public beaches. But as I drove past the park I was

Chinese Urine Pot

Chamber Pot

Some type of pot has been used as a toilet since ancient time. Roman slaves would bring urine pots for diners to use during dinner parties.

Household that had privies outside usually also had chamber pots inside for night use. In wealthy households chamber pots were cleaned by slaves or servants.

In poorer homes chamber pots were usually hidden, either in a cupboard or under the bed. In wealthier homes they were hidden in commodes - a sort of cabinet which often also contained a wash basin, jug, soap dish and slop bowl.

Modern commodes are a chair with a chamber pot set into the seat.

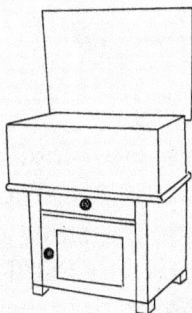

Antique Commode Cabinet

Modern Commode Chair

mystified to see signs pointing to places to visit in the park, but with warnings on the signs that there would be "no sanitary facilities". The facilities that were provided in the park appeared to almost all be "seasonal restrooms". The assumption seemed to be that the Cape Cod park visitors either had no toileting needs, or only seasonal ones.

I stopped and went for one of the scenic walks in the beautiful park and the inevitable happened - I needed to have a pee. When the feeling became urgent and physically painful, I had to find some foliage to hide in while I blissfully relieved myself.

In Massachusetts I caused a bit of embarrassment at the Plymouth Plantation. It is south of Boston and is a replica of life at Plymouth in the 1600s. I asked both the Pilgrims and the Indians at the Plantation to tell me where people went to the toilet in the 1600s. I don't like our sanitised way of discussing how people lived in past times - I always wonder where they went to the toilet.

The Indian elder told me most Indians just went in the woods, but not near water. Also the Indian men urinated around their crops as the smell deterred the deer and wildlife from the crops. The Pilgrims also used the woods for a toilet. However, if they were in a hurry, or did not want to go to the woods, they used their chamber pots. Some would then empty the chamber pot in the nearby woods. Most just threw their chamber pot contents into the street outside their house for the pigs to eat.

In Australia, I have suffered two different misfortunes from using the woods (called the bush) as a toilet. The Australian bush is no idyllic place. We have more deadly poisonous critters than anywhere else in the world. The east coast bush is infested with ticks. These are small blood sucking parasites about the size of a flea. Ticks attach themselves to your skin, where they can stay for days. One Australian type of tick can cause paralysis and death to humans and animals.

A number of countries have traditionally disposed of human manure by giving it to pigs to eat. Archaeologists have found models of ancient Chinese toilets built above pig pens. The Chinese models show men and women used different toilets.

My first misfortune was to find, many hours after having a pee in the bush, that I had a tick attached to my genitals. One does not just brush a tick off, because they bury their heads into your skin. Getting the tick removed was a difficult and rather embarrassing process. It was not long after the tick incident that I had my second misfortune going to the toilet in the bush. I was in rain forest and I did not know then that rain forests are infested with blood sucking leeches. I thought leeches were something used by quacks in past centuries to draw blood in the hope of curing illness.

This time, many hours after going to the toilet, I found a swollen, blood engorged leech attached to my genitals. Fortunately, the leech was easier to remove than the tick.

WORLD TRAVEL AND A HISTORY OF TOILETS

ChapterTwo
Rotten Peaches For Dessert

A week after I had visited the Plymouth Plantation and said goodbye to Cyril, I was in an historic wool spinning mill in Yorkshire in the United Kingdom. The rules for the 18th century mill workers were on display. These included guidelines about visits to the "necessity". Initially I wondered what the "necessity" was, but after reading all the rules I concluded it must be the toilet. One of the rules was that if a male worker was found any where near the female "necessity", he would be instantly dismissed.

I was staying not far away from Yorkshire in a bed and breakfast lodging in the scenic Lake District. My toilet was in my very public, supposedly

In the western world privies were widely used before modern toilet plumbing was developed. A privy consisted of a small outhouse (sometimes called a "necessity") containing a wooden toilet seat above a large circular hole (the privy pit).

More expensive privy pits were lined with brick or stone. They could be 20 feet (or 6 metres) deep. Cheaper privy pits were shallower and unlined, or lined with wood.

Pollution could easily leak out of a pit, often into a nearby water well or other drinking water supply.

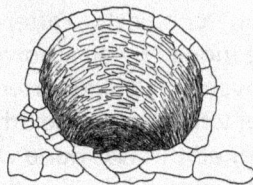

Privy Pit

private, bathroom. When I booked the accommodation I had been assured I would have a private bathroom.

When I arrived at the lodging I found that my bathroom was some distance away from my bedroom and it was located half way up a staircase, which everyone in the house frequently used. There were rules posted on the wall of my bedroom. The rules told me I had to wear the supplied robe and slippers when I visited my bathroom. When in my bathroom I had to lock the door and lower the blind. They also said I had to raise the blind again before leaving the bathroom. I did not wear the robe or slippers and I kept forgetting the blind routine.

The Groom of the Stool was an important position in the English court. It was usually filled by an ambitious nobleman (or noblewoman if a queen was reigning). In Medieval times one of the key duties of the Groom of the Stool was to wipe clean the monarch's bottom after the monarch had a bowel movement. It is reported that when Henry the 8th reigned this was done with the Groom of the Stool's hand.

From the Lake District I travelled to Nice in France. Unlike the Americans in Massachusetts, it appeared the French in Nice needed to go frequently. There were lots of clearly marked toilets. There were also an amazing number of very cute little dogs, who were walked several times a day, because they lived in apartments. The sidewalks were covered in dog shit. Unfortunately, I trod in a freshly laid pile, which must have belonged to a larger dog.

In Nice I stayed with Madame Buffet as a boarder in her elegant apartment, which was close to the beach. Madame was mean with money. This was not from necessity. She owned four properties in Nice that were worth a huge amount of money and from which she received a good income. Nevertheless, she slept on a sofa in the small dining room in her apartment, so she could rent out her bedroom to language students, such as I was. Madame also liked to do her own repairs.

In Medieval times people living in towns and cities went to the toilet in a pot and then threw the contents into the street. In some places you had to shout a warning before you did this.

"Loo" - a modern slang word for toilet - probably was derived from the warning "gardy-loo". That term came from the French "garde de l'eau" (beware of the water).

Medieval Sewerage Disposal

When I first leant back in the wooden chair in my bedroom I was alarmed that the back started parting from the chair. By quickly leaning forward again I just managed to save myself from a nasty accident. Close inspection of the chair revealed that the back was just clumsily glued on to the chair seat. The glue had long ago given up holding strongly.

Lots of things have been used for toilet paper. The ancient Romans used sponges on sticks. Different cultures have used wool, fabric, leaves, corn cobs, wood, moss or their left hand. In China paper has been used for fourteen centuries. In the Ming Dynasty the Imperial family's toilet paper was soft and perfumed. Paper was not used in the West until much later than it was used in China.

In the West newspaper and magazine pages were used before modern toilet paper was developed. Toilet paper rolls like we use today were first made in the late eighteen hundreds. Amazingly, it took quite a few more years until toilet paper was splinter free.

The apartment's toilet was in a not very clean bathroom. Madame sometimes washed the floor with dirty water that just made the floor even dirtier. When I tried to put a new toilet roll on the empty holder, the holder fell off the wall. It was another of Madame's shoddy repairs. The holder was not properly attached to the wall - tiny screws had been used instead of ones the appropriate size for the large screw holes. I put the toilet roll holder back on the wall as best I could using the same little screws. I did this because Madame got most disappointed and resentful when I pointed out to her that something needed fixing. She always seemed to pay me back for complaining by doing things like giving me curdled milk for my breakfast tea, or rotten peaches for dessert at night.

However, Madame Buffet did provide toilet paper that was of reasonable quality. I remember when I was in my early twenties and staying in London, the hotels had ridiculous toilet paper. It was hard, densely woven and glossy. I am not sure what you were supposed to do with it because it was hopeless for its intended function.

While in Nice I took a trip on a small private train which runs from Nice to Digne - where the lavender grows. It was a three and half hour journey.

Quite a lot of old castles had toilets that protruded from the side of the castle. The waste from such toilets would drop straight from them into water, such as a moat, below. The waste from the protruding toilets at Olavinlinna Castle in Finland would drop about 20 metres into water below. Some old houses also had a protruding toilet. Waste would fall on to the ground, or into water.

Olavinlinna Castle Toilet

The toilet on the train was one of those old sorts where what you do drops straight on to the ground between the train tracks. At least, after the stuffy train carriage, there was a draft of cold air on your backside when you sat on the toilet.

I stayed in Digne for the day and went to the public toilet there before leaving on the last train. It was unisex and you paid to go in. The attendant was a snappily dressed young French woman. I wondered what it would be like to have her job. I wouldn't like to listen to and smell people going to the toilet all day, day after day, but I guess we all do the best we can in life.

In contemporary Japan many Japanese women do not want other people listening to them going to the toilet. Therefore, many public toilets are fitted with electronic devices called Sound Princesses.

The device allows women to mask the sounds they are making in the toilet - the sounds of them urinating, passing wind or faeces. They activate the device and it produces the sound of flushing, even though the toilet is not flushing.

It is also not very pleasant having someone listening to you go to the toilet. I once did a few days consultancy work in a defence establishment. Because the establishment had a top security classification I was provided with a male escort. He went everywhere with me. This included standing outside my toilet door while I went. It was very off putting.

The meanest toilet I ever went to had a French connection. It was in the French territory of New Caledonia and it was a public toilet. An attendant was constantly hosing the floor with water. You paid your money to enter and you were given one tiny scrap of toilet paper to take in with you.

WORLD TRAVEL AND A HISTORY OF TOILETS

Chapter Three
Squatting On The Rim

After 3 weeks in Nice, I spent a week driving from the south of France to Charleville-Mezieres in the north. Initially I drove on the main toll-ways, which were sufficiently provided with stops where you could buy petrol, get food or go to the toilet.

Sometimes a women's toilet at a toll-way stop included a clearly labelled cubicle for Turkish women. These cubicles did not contain a normal pedestal toilet. Instead, they had a small hole in the floor, which had a footprint marked either side to indicate where to put your feet as you squatted over the hole.

For some reason, one of the stops did not have any pedestal toilets at all, only toilets for Turkish women. I avoided these type of toilets as they were usually very unpleasant, having urine and water splashed around on the floor. I can not imagine how women wearing traditional clothing manage to stop some

Sign Warning Toilet Users Not To Squat Over A Western Toilet

of their long, baggy garments dragging in the smelly wet as they squatted.

Traditional Japanese toilets were squatting type toilets. These toilets can be difficult for Westerners as their muscles are not use to the squat position. On the other hand, many Japanese initially thought that Western seat type toilets were disgusting. This was because the user's bare bottom sat on a seat that lots of other bare bottoms had sat on. Rather than sit on the toilet seat, some Japanese would raise it and then precariously squat on the rim of the toilet pedestal.

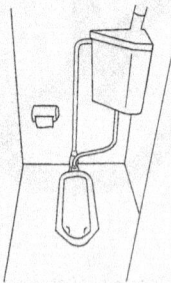

Japanese Squat Toilet

After a couple of days driving on the toll-ways, I decided to leave them and drive along the smaller back roads. I could see more of the countryside, and also not be charged expensive tolls. I only have one complaint about my delightful drive, and it is a serious one. Once you were out of the cities and off the main toll-ways, there was an almost complete lack of toilets, including in the villages. There were ample road side stops, often with trees and benches, but no toilets. I compensated for this difficulty by drinking little, and stopping wherever I could go discretely for a pee.

At one road side stop that did not have a toilet, I went into the bushes to pee. I accidentally trod on someone's shit and I found the area littered with toilet paper. Clearly I was not the only one to have the problem of no toilet, nor to seek the solution exactly where I did. For the rest of my cross-country drive I had to use my ingenuity, which included having a pee behind a church buttress in central France, and in northern France behind a monument to the dead of WWI .

France gains a lot of revenue from its 75 million tourists a year. To encourage tourism, a huge amount of money is spent on flowers, but very little is spent on public toilets. Just as hotels are awarded stars, villages compete to be awarded flowers. A three flower village is a fantastic sight - flowers grow on bridges, flowers grow on widow sills, flowers grow everywhere.

In 2,500BC the Harappa civilisation in India used water to carry away the sewerage from the toilets in their houses. This was done by brick covered drains that had inspection man-holes.

As early as 2,000BC the Egyptians had seat type toilets. A bowl of sand might be placed under the seat to catch the waste.

One of the oldest examples of a toilet that was flushed clean by water was in the ancient Minoan palace of Knossos in Crete. In 1,500BC water was stored in reservoir in the palace roof so that it could flush the toilet below.

Unfortunately, when these ancient civilisations declined their sanitary engineering also disappeared.

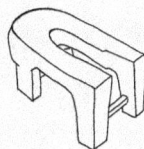

Ancient Egyption Toliet Seat

At Charleville-Mezieres I joined a small barge for a week of cruising on the spectacular River Meuse canal. I had one of the two guests' cabins. My cabin had quite a roomy bathroom, which contained a bath, a hand basin and a toilet.

When I joined the cruise, Kevin, the barge captain, told me a lot of rules. His toilet rule was that I was only

The ancient Romans had well designed toilets. They often used flowing water underneath their toilets to take away the waste, via sewers which discharged the untreated waste straight into rivers.

They built large public toilets. While using these toilets people sat next to each other on benches. The design of the toilets allowed them to be sat on, or men could stand in front of them and urinate into them. A channel of water ran in front of a toilet bench, so that toilet users could wash their hands.

One famous example of this style of toilet was in Ephesus where it can still be visited today. It had thirty six stone seats. Slaves were sometimes used to sit on a seat first to warm it up.

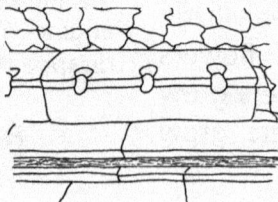

Ephesus Toilet

allowed to put into the toilet what I had eaten. All my used toilet paper had to go into a little bin by my toilet. Kevin told me that each day I was to discretely empty the little bin into the kitchen sink. I looked so horrified when he told me this, that he corrected himself and said to empty it into the larger kitchen bin, not the kitchen sink.

The second time I used my toilet, I forgot the rule and flushed my piece of toilet paper away. I knew immediately I had broken the rule and I felt guilty. I hoped the crewman, Yoseff, who was working on the deck above my cabin, had not noticed. He could have easily noticed because all the sewerage from our barge, and all the other boats, went straight into the river. I was shocked that the river would be fouled in such a way.

The toilet in an ancient sailing ship was usually a plank with hole in it at the front of the ship, or "the head". It was placed there so that waste could easily drop into the sea and the splashing water would keep the toilet area clean. There was no privacy when sailors used the toilet.

In 1858 the River Thames was so polluted, especially with sewerage, that the House of Commons had to be abandoned because of the stench. The fish in the river died and the birds that fed off them either died or left.

The smell during the hot and humid summer was known as "the great stink". The stench, and the realisation that the contamination caused cholera, led to the engineering feat of the building of an effective London sewerage system.

I recall that the foulest toilet I ever visited was when I was on quite an expensive tour of north Thailand. Part of the tour was lunch at a restaurant near the River Kwai. After lunch, in order to answer the call of nature, I had to visit a stinking hovel behind the restaurant building and stand in about ten centimetres of urine and shit that was sloshing around on the floor.

Throughout history being a prisoner or slave could mean enduring a lack of sanitary conditions. For example, the slaves on board the slave ships during the Trans-atlantic slave trade suffered appalling conditions. They were shackled and tightly packed below deck.

Some captains just let the slaves lay in their collective foul smelling excreta for the whole trip, which could take several months. Other captains provided some buckets (although many slaves did not try to use the buckets because they were too difficult to reach) and had regular cleaning of the slaves' quarters.

Hot or stormy weather made the stinking conditions worse as the slaves might also vomit or bleed.

It was a horrible and disgusting experience, and rather an incomprehensible one. It was a rural area and there was plenty of space, surely such filth was unnecessary - why did people live like that? It is as inexplicable as the Western Australian café that served me a toasted cheese sandwich with the plastic wrappers still on the slice of melted cheese.

I had some other trouble when travelling in Western Australia. I was touring the beautiful south west when I had to stop at a not very clean public toilet to answer the call of nature. I was elegantly dressed and wearing a necklace of opal beads. It was a rare and expensive piece of jewellery. When I had finished going to the toilet I stood up, turned around, and lent over the toilet pan to flush the toilet. At that precise moment my necklace broke and most of the opal beads fell into the toilet pan.

I took quite a while to decide whether to put my hand into the toilet and fish around in my waste and retrieve the beads, or just flush the toilet and lose the expensive and unique beads. It is amazing what we can do when we have to.

WORLD TRAVEL AND A HISTORY OF TOILETS

Chapter Four
Unrefined Habits

After my week of lazily cruising on the barge I went to Exeter College at Oxford University to do an intensive three week course. Oxford is a city with a long history of drunken carousing. When I walked around the streets on Sunday morning it was not uncommon to find vomit on the pavement, or a used condom down by the river - the leftovers of the previous night's excesses.

At Exeter College the ornate, stone building I lived in was very old. I was privileged to be given the rooms that Tolkien, author of The Lord Of The Rings, used to live in when he was a student at Exeter. But the rooms were at the top of many flights of narrow winding stairs and the shared toilet was quite problematic.

For the first three days I was there I constantly fell in or out of the toilet doorway because of a seven inches high (or 18 centimetres if you are metric) obstruction on the floor of the doorway. The floor of the small toilet room was actually a metal tray, the edges of which extended upward into the doorway, creating the obstruction. As you don't normally stare

Since ancient times various types of condoms have been worn on the penis during sex to help prevent infection or pregnancy. Early condoms were made from:

- fabric (such as linen or silk)
- leather
- animal guts (such as goats' bladders or sheep's intestine)
- fish membranes

Some early condoms were expensive, ill fitting and strong smelling; however, most could be used again after washing and drying.

Linen condoms were sometimes soaked in solutions (such as salt and herbs) that were thought to assist in disease prevention. The open end of a condom usually had a ribbon which could be used to tie the condom in place.

Condoms made of rubber became available in the 19th Century. The early rubber condoms broke easily unless they were made unreasonably thick. Eventually a new process allowed very thin latex condoms to be made. These "rubbers" were packaged in small tins which have become collectors' items.

Today condoms can be made from synthetic materials and they also come in a wide variety of textures, shapes, colours and flavours.

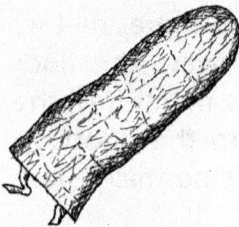

Early Linen Condom

Modern Condom

at the floor when you go through a doorway, I kept forgetting the obstruction and tripping over it.

I had a very unpleasant sound experience in another Exeter College toilet situated near the lecture theatre. There was mercifully no obstruction on the floor of the doorway, but there was a dodgey door lock. When you wanted to leave the toilet cubicle it often took several minutes to get the door open, because the lock would stick.

It was bad luck that I was in the toilet doing my business, when a lengthy fire siren test began. There was a speaker directly above my head and from it came the most horrible, high pitched sound I've ever heard. The ancient building was a serious fire hazard because of all the timber and air spaces in it. If a fire started the building would burn very quickly, so the warning siren was especially loud.

Before I could flee from the excruciating noise, I had to

Menstrual blood has been used for many purposes, including magic practices. In the ancient Greco-Roman world it was sometimes used for healing purposes such as a supposed cure for sores or malaria. Bracelets with threads that had been soaked in menstrual blood were thought to stop fevers.

In the middle ages it was thought to cure leprosy. It has also often been used as a fertiliser for plants. In some cultures women have to go into seclusion whilst menstruating.

Throughout history women have used different materials to absorb menstrual blood. However, some women do not use any methods to effective absorb it, usually because of poverty.

Tampons inserted into the vagina have been used to absorb menstrual blood. Women in Africa and Asia have made tampons from plants, grasses and mosses. In the ancient world Egyptian women had soft papyrus tampons, Roman women had wool tampons and Japanese women had paper tampons. In the early twentieth century some western women wore tampons made from rolled surgical cotton or sea sponges.

While a high percentage of western women wear tampons today, only a small percentage of the global population of women do.

first finish doing my business. That done, when I tried to leave the small toilet cubicle, the lock stuck. I could not open the door. I became worried that the lock had finally completely failed. Thankfully, after several minutes of trying, I managed to get the door open and fled from the horrific noise.

The other students doing the course at Oxford University were from various countries in the world, and almost all were mature age students. Unhappily, they weren't all refined with their toileting habits.

I was lucky that those with whom I shared my toilet were reasonably clean. My friend Patricia, who was staying in a different part of the college, was not so lucky. She was from ritzy Newport in the United States and she was appalled to keep finding a mess of bloody toilet paper on the floor of her shared toilet. It had been thrown there by a woman who was menstruating, instead of being flushed away in the toilet, or put in the toilet bin.

Patricia complained to the course Professor who had a dignified sign put up in the toilet. The sign politely asked users to leave the toilet as tidy as they had found it. The sign had no effect. Patricia then put up a much more explicit sign which, amongst other things, told the perpetrator how gross they were. Patricia's sign was effective.

While I was staying at Oxford University I took the opportunity to visit the nearby ostentatious Blenheim Palace, the ancestral home of the wealthy Dukes of Marlborough. The Palace is famous both

Pads have also been and are still used to externally absorb menstrual blood. These have been made of similar materials to tampons. American women used to wear a type of nappy made out of absorbent fabric until the nineteen twenties. They washed and reused the nappies. Then pads became widely used. Originally they were held in place by a belt. Modern pads stick on to women's panties.

Today silicone menstrual cups are also available. A cup is worn internally in the vagina and it collects the blood. The cup is removed, emptied, washed and then replaced two to three times a day.

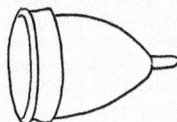

Menstrual Cup

for being Winston Churchill's birthplace and for its magnificent gardens.

When touring the palace I saw a Marlborough crested chamber pot proudly on display. I was amazed to learn that the Duke (of the time) did not stop using a chamber pot until just before World War II. If I had that fabulous wealth the last thing I would want to be using would be a chamber pot. I much prefer the greater delicacy of flushing toilets.

I remember moving to Sydney in 1969 and being horrified to discover that some suburbs still did not have flushing toilets. Instead people used a large bucket placed under a wooden bench which had a toilet seat cut into it. The buckets were only emptied once a week, when collection carts came at night to pick up the "night soil".

Because the buckets stank so much they were in outhouses, which were small sheds in backyards. Visiting those toilets in winter was generally a very cold and unpleasant experience. The toilets looked and smelt awful, particularly if their buckets were full and due to be emptied.

Because the first manned American space flight was only for 15 minutes, it was assumed the astronaut would not need to go to the toilet. However, the launch was delayed and the astronaut had to spend many hours waiting in the rocket, lying on his back. He eventually urinated in his space suit.

The second astronaut wore a large nappy. As flights got longer better solutions were needed. The main problem being that in outer space there is a lack of gravity. If a normal toilet was used, bodily wastes would float in the air.

The next solution was to stick a plastic bag onto an astronaut's bottom. After he had been to the toilet, he had to grab his faeces through the bag, remove the bag and roll it up. There were some occasions when, before the astronaut could roll up the bag, his faeces floated out of it.

Now space shuttles have toilets which flush with air. An astronaut sits on a toilet in a tiny little room. Because of the gravity problem, the astronaut has to be held in place by restraints. Air is used to push faeces away from the astronaut's bottom into a bag. The faeces is brought back to earth for analysis.

Both male and female astronauts can use the urinal. It is a funnel on a flexible hose which uses air to force the urine into a collector. Occasionally the stored urine is emptied into space.

WORLD TRAVEL AND A HISTORY OF TOILETS

Chapter Five
The Witch Will Get Them

After my Oxford course finished I visited the famous Cotswold district, which has lots of historic thatched cottages. I stayed in a bed and breakfast lodging in Bourton on the Water - a pretty little village with a river flowing through its centre. The house I stayed in was full of dolls - hundreds of them. They were crammed into every nook and cranny, in some rooms a huge mass of them was tiered right up a wall to the ceiling.

A rule posted on my bedroom wall told me, in order not to inconvenience other people, I could not have a bath between 10pm and 7.30am. My bedroom did not have an en-suite bathroom. I had to use a shared bathroom, which contained a very annoying toilet. It was annoying because most of the time it would not flush.

I thought that the bed and breakfast owners' priorities were odd. Finding an unflushed toilet would have been far more inconvenient to most people, than someone else having a bath at 10pm.

There is an international toilet museum in India - the Sulabh Museum. It displays toilets which show the evolution of toilet design.

After some determined experimentation I worked out how to make it flush. I had to remove the cistern lid and then manually lift the mechanism that made water flow into the toilet bowl. This was a wet and frustrating procedure, because it usually took a few attempts before I could get the water to flush the toilet.

Today the Japanese make very high tech toilets which can include the following features in their design:

- arm rests
- automatic lid
- glowing in the dark
- seat heating
- air conditioning below the rim
- germ resisting surfaces
- automatic flushing and air deodorising

Current developments include:

- operation by voice activation
- measuring blood sugar, pulse, blood pressure and body fat with medical sensors
- giving enemas
- giving sexual pleasure

When I left the United Kingdom, on my way home to Australia, I stopped for a few days in India. I ended up having a tantrum in a Mumbai airport lounge and told the attendant it was the lounge from hell. The lounge purported to be a comfortable waiting area with good facilities for business and first class passengers. The reality was the lounge was small, uncomfortable and poorly serviced.

It served a number of different airlines at the same time. Hordes came to it - Indians, Arabs, Westerners

- families, individuals, couples. Children fought, screamed, rolled on the floor and wall televisions blared. While staring pointedly at me, a burkha-clad Middle Eastern woman threatened her riotous young boys that if they did not behave the witch would get them and lock them in a dark cellar.

Passengers were turned away from the small lounge because there was no room for them to come into it. Many were outraged and argued at the door. The packed horrible lounge, meant for the wealthier travellers, only had one female toilet cubicle.

When I left the lounge to go to my plane I walked past the economy passengers waiting area. The economy passengers had chaise-lounge chairs which allowed them to recline in comfort. The area was quite peaceful and not at all crowded. It was adequately provided with toilets. As the

In Japan during the second half of the nineteenth century both men and women used urinals. Women wore kimonos without underwear underneath. To use the urinal, a woman would lift her kimono and pull her vulva area upwards. She could then direct her stream of urine into the urinal.

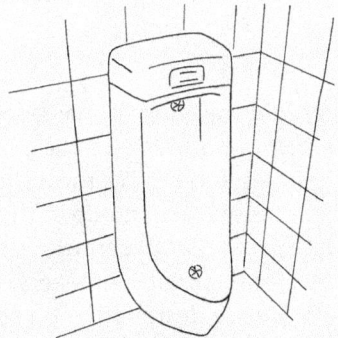

Urinal

Indian tourism promotion adverts say "India is an incredible place!"

My flight home to Australia was uneventful, but I was very pleased I was not flying economy. Soon after we took off from India, two of the economy passengers' toilets had to be closed for the whole flight because passengers had been sick in them.

This reminded me that a few years ago a flight of Japanese tourists returning home to Japan from Australia all got gastro during the flight. They got it from the airline food they were served. It must have been a horrific flight. Just a few toilets and a plane load of people all vomiting and with diarrhoea!

A bidet traditionally has been a sort of basin for washing genitals and the bottom. The first bidets were made in the late seventeenth century by French furniture makers. They were designed to be sat astride as if riding a horse.

17th Century Bidet

Today some countries have bidets, others do not. Therefore, many people do not know what a bidet is, or how to use it. People who have never seen a modern bidet before often mistake it for a toilet, or a drinking fountain!!!

There are two main types of modern bidets. One bidet design is a china basin which is separate to a toilet. This bidet can have either taps for filling the basin with water, or a nozzle which sprays a jet of water.

The second type of bidet is incorporated into the toilet. This type has either one nozzle or two nozzles that spray water. One nozzle is short and meant for cleaning the bottom. The second nozzle is longer and meant for cleaning women's genitals. Some have only one nozzle, but it can angle its jet of water to suit either function.

Some modern bidets have a pulsating and massaging water jet setting. They also have a warm air drying function.

Modern Bidet

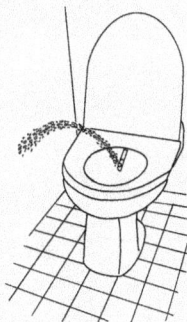

Combined Toilet/Biget

WORLD TRAVEL AND A HISTORY OF TOILETS

WORLD TRAVEL AND A HISTORY OF TOILETS

www.ingramcontent.com/pod-product-compliance
Lightning Source LLC
Chambersburg PA
CBHW070110070426
42448CB00038B/2495